Zooming the Zoo

To Jen, who keeps me going.
To Noah & Cara, of course.
And to the Wednesday Poets, without whom
this book would probably be half the length.
J.D.

To Roy Castle and Natasha Kinsella
T.M-J.

Text copyright © John Dougherty 2024
Illustrations copyright © Tom Morgan-Jones 2024
The right of John Dougherty and Tom Morgan-Jones to be identified as the author and illustrator of this work has been asserted by them in accordance with the Copyright, Designs and Patents Act, 1988 (United Kingdom).

First published in Great Britain and in the USA in 2024 by
Otter-Barry Books, Little Orchard, Burley Gate, Herefordshire, HR1 3QS
www.otterbarrybooks.com

A catalogue record for this book is available from the British Library.

Designed by Arianna Osti

ISBN 978-1-915659-21-7

Illustrated with a dip pen and ink

Set in Warnock Pro

Printed in Great Britain

9 8 7 6 5 4 3 2 1

Zooming the Zoo

Poems by
John Dougherty

Illustrated by
Tom Morgan-Jones

Otter-Barry BOOKS

CONTENTS

Poetry Rules 6

Zooming the Zoo 8

Morning Poem 10

When You're a Kid 11

The Cruel and Unfair Rule About Hair 12

Miss Ran the Marathon 15

Grandad and the Deckchair 16

Blessu 18

Texting Haiku on the Tube 18

Apparently my Haiku Are Not Proper Haiku 18

It's Sometimes OK 19

Rover Loves to Chew Things 20

Break 22

A Clerihew About Clerihews 24

Clerihew About a Word I Find
Unexpectedly Difficult to Say 24

Two Clerihews About Clara Hughes 25

Dickens and Doyle 26

Cardi B 26

David Attenborough 27

What Happened to the Dinosaur? 28

Beware of the Leotard 29

The Ghosts of Grizzerley Grange 30

A Poem About Something Small 34

Just Let Me Read 35

Jade and Joe 36

Lions in Love 40

Excuses 42

I Did Do My Homework 44

Blank Verse 46

The World is Too Much Sometimes 47

Rainbows and Steel 48

Snowfall	49
I Am a Man of Naughtiness	50
Limerick Written by a Dog	52
A Serious and Thought-Provoking Poem Written by a Dog	53
If I Were a Bear	53
Let Down Your Hair	54
If Somebody Hurts You	56
How to Write a Cinquain	58
I Would Not Like to Be a Slug	59
Robinswood Hill	60
Unexpected Item	61
Boys Will Be Boys	62
There is a Poem	63
Onomatopoeia Poem	64
The Dog's Not Allowed on the Chair	66
Computer Poem	68
Pity the Bat	69
The Problem with Acrostics	70
Steps	71
What Kind of Poem is This?	72
Our Minds Are Made of Play-Dough	73
Cough	74
Calorie Mentality	76
Zoos – Good or Bad?	78
In the Library	80
Poet	82
Goodbye, Grandad	83
Learning to Walk	84
The First Time I Went to Scotland	85
Taking My Children to Larne	90
Yellow Group	92
You Are You	94
About the Poet and the Illustrator	96

Poetry Rules

Poetry rules
Even though it has none
But if you need some...

Rule one:
have fun

Rule two:
do what you want to do

Rule three:
set your imagination free

Rule four:
there aren't any more

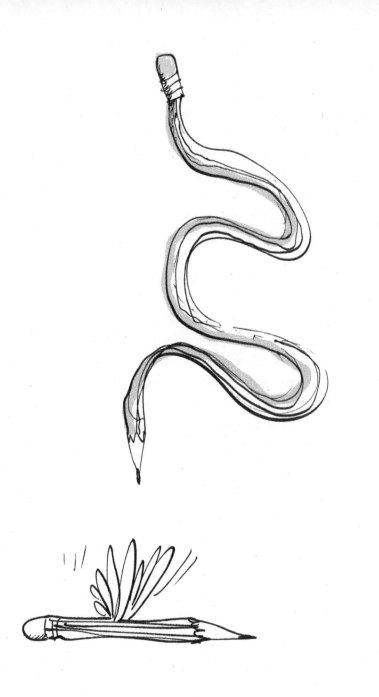

Zooming the Zoo

Suggesting this zoo held a meeting on Zoom
Was not sensible, wise or astute
For the sloths all appear to be frozen onscreen
And I think that the swan's stuck on mute

There's a fault with the mic in the reptile house
It's making an odd sort of hissing
And although all their webcams are working okay
The chameleons seem to be missing

I've had to disable the chat function, too
For they just don't seem able to cope with it
And the antelopes all have signed out of the call
For the lions are being... inappropriate

So I think that I'm going to abandon this Zoom call
I'll give up and go back to bed
And next time I'm tempted to hold a zoo meeting
We'll do it on FaceTime instead.

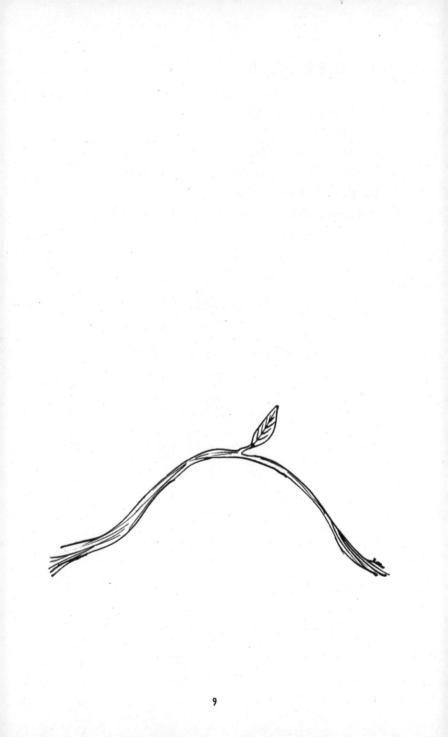

Morning Poem

This is my morning poem
A stretch, a yawn
A word to greet the day
A shaking off of all the sleepy "Leave me here"s
The "I can't"s and "It's too early"s
A flinging wide of the back door of my imagination
To let the sunlight in.

When You're a Kid

When you're a kid
You can sit on the lid
Of the toilet, facing the cistern
Revving the handle
Pretending
You're on a motorbike
And the flushing sound
Is the powerful roar of the engine.

When you're a teacher
You can't.

The Cruel and Unfair Rule About Hair

When I was at school
they had rules
about hair
that weren't fair.
For why shouldn't boys wear it long?
It seemed wrong
when the girls were allowed to
and taught to be proud to,
while the boys had to wear
our hair
so short that our necks were visible
even if it made us miserable.

But one day, a lad
came to school, and he'd had
his head shaved completely.
And though it had been done neatly,
the Head sent him home
till his hair had regrown.

Which seemed so unfair that it left us appalled –
for the Head himself
was totally bald.

Miss Ran the Marathon

Miss ran the marathon!
We can't believe it –
Miss! Our Miss,
who never takes exercise when she can take a taxi,
who thinks she's eaten a balanced meal if her second helping
weighs the same as the first,
who brings in notes from her mum explaining why she
can't teach PE.

And she finished it! Twenty-six miles and a little bit more
in less than a weekend!

Now she's sitting at the front of the class,
feet up, looking all pleased with herself
and saying,
"You lot better be good today,
or I'll take my socks off
and show you my blisters!"

Grandad and the Deckchair

We left Grandad wrestling a deckchair
He wanted to lie in the sun
But when we came back minutes later
The deckchair had won.

There wasn't a sign of poor Grandad
Except for his cap on the floor
The deckchair just grinned and let out a burp
Then lay down and started to snore.

Blessu

A hai... hai... hai... hai...............
A hai-hai... A-hai-hai-hai..........
A hai-hai-haiku!!

Texting Haiku on the Tube

The unsent haiku
There is no mobile signal
On the Circle Line

Apparently My Haiku Are Not Proper Haiku

"That's not a haiku"
People say, in Japanese
I don't understand

It's Sometimes Okay

It's sometimes okay
To not feel all "Yay!"
It's sometimes okay to be glum
There are days when the world
Is a bracelet of pearls
And days it's a pain in the bum

Rover Loves to Chew Things

Rover loves to chew things
He loves to tear and gnaw
He loves to pull things with his teeth
As he holds them with his paw

He chews my socks, he chews my shoes
He chews the cushions, too
He'll chew through anything, except
The things we let him chew

I gave the dog a chewy toy
I gave the dog a bone
But Rover loves the oven glove
And he won't leave it alone

I gave the dog some tasty treats
That he could chew instead
But Rover seems to much prefer
The mattress on my bed

I gave the dog a rubber ring
A lovely stick, and more
But Rover just ignored them all
And chewed right through the floor

And then he kept on going
Much to my regret
I miss him chewing up my house
Now I fear he's reached Tibet.

Break

There's a vaulting horse in the playground
and teachers, break-time cups of tea forgotten,
are leaping over it, one after another after another.

Along comes the visitor,
the school inspector, who we've all been told
we have to be especially nice to.

He asks what they're doing.
"Just exercising," says Miss Jones,
"just exercising."

But from under the horse
there's a noise that sounds suspiciously like tunnelling
and no one's seen the Head all morning.

A Clerihew About Clerihews

Writing a clerihew
Is not very hard to do
Since, as far as I recall
The length of the lines really doesn't matter very much at all

Clerihew About a Word that I Find Unexpectedly Difficult to Say

The word 'Japanese'
I can pronounce with ease
But saying 'multiplication'
Requires concentration

Two Clerihews About Clara Hughes

Clara Hughes
Would rather you didn't confuse
Her with a limerick, or worse
With this particular style of verse.

Clara Hughes
Doesn't like to lose.
Before she was terribly old
She won an Olympic gold.*

*And several other medals. Look her up; she's quite impressive.

Dickens and Doyle

Charles Dickens
Liked to eat chickens
But Sir Arthur Conan Doyle
Preferred to eat soil

Cardi B

Cardi B
Is stylish, you'll agree
But it should not be forgotten
That her full name is Cardigan Button

David Attenborough

David Attenborough
Knew the Latin for a
Lot of names of animal species
Which he taught to his nephews and niecies

What Happened to the Dinosaur?

What happened to the dinosaur?
Perhaps you haven't heard
But science has a theory
Though I know it sounds absurd
That evolution changed its shape
From dinosaur to bird

So if you saw a dinosaur
Would you run and hide?
Or cover it with herbs & spice
And have it southern-fried
With chips and beans and garden peas
And ketchup on the side?

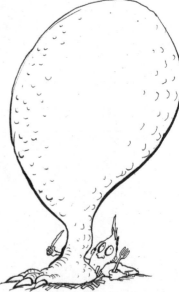

Beware of the Leotard

The sign said, *Beware of the leotard.*
'Surely that should be *leopard*?' I
thought,
just before an angry big cat leapt out
at me
and performed a ferocious piece of
interpretive dance.

The Ghosts of Grizzerley Grange

In Grizzerley Grange you'll hear noises most strange
If you're there in the dead of the night
And the locals will say, don't be tempted to stay
Or you're likely to perish from fright
You'll hear nightmarish screams that will haunt all
    your dreams
And unspeakable murmurings too
But most fearful of all is the terrible call
Of the Grizzerley ghosts going
ooOOOOOOOOOOOoooooo

As you go up the stair you'll hear somebody there
But your eyes will see nothing at all
You'll hear footsteps resounding; your heart will start
    pounding
As echoes drift up from the hall
There'll be pitiful moans and quite ominous groans
And a sound like the turn of a screw
But more scary than these is the wail on the breeze
Of the Grizzerley ghosts going
ooOOOOOOOOOOOoooooo

There'll be sounds quite as frightening as thunder and
    lightning
The flickering light will go out
In the dark of your room there will come through the gloom
A crash and a menacing shout
You'll hear creaking and squeaking and somebody speaking
In tones that will chill you right through
But the sound you'll most fear is the sigh in your ear
Of the Grizzerley ghosts going
ooOOOOOOOOOOOooooo

Though your heart turns to frost, though you feel all
    is lost
Don't give in to your fears, or forget
That although they alarm you, they can't touch or
    harm you
Their noises are nothing but threat
There's a reason that they want to scare you away
It may sound absurd, but it's true
If you're breathing and living and loving and giving
The ghosts are more frightened of
    y-ooOOOOOOOOOOOooooo

A Poem About Something Small

I need to write
A little poem
About something small
So here's my plan

I'm going to write
A little poem
About
My concentr...

Just Let Me Read

Just let me read
Without counting commas
Identifying idioms
Noticing nouns
Analysing analogies

Let me feel a sense of wonder
Without asking me to wonder
How it was achieved

There will be time
When my head is full of stories
So full
They pour from my pen
Then
There will be time
To look behind the curtain
To see the smoke, the mirrors
The tricks that make the magic
But until then
Please

Just let me read.

Jade and Joe

Jade's a girl
Who climbs up trees
Who skins her hands
And scrapes her knees
Who tackles bullies
Won't give way
Says the things
She wants to say
Plays up front
Loves to score
See her shoot
And hear her roar
It's who she is
It's how she's made
Jade's a girl
And this is Jade.

Joe's a boy
Who's sweet and caring
Kindly, generous
And sharing
Likes to dance
Loves to sing
Really good
At listening
Paints his nails
Grows his hair
Is quietly and simply
There
It's who he is
This much we know
Joe's a boy
And this is Joe.

Sometimes people
Like to say
That girls should be
A certain way
While boys are different
So they claim
All girls alike
All boys the same
But that's untrue
Don't be afraid
Let Joe be Joe
Let Jade be Jade

Let me be me
Let you be you

Let each one to ourselves be true.

Lions in Love

In the heart of the vast Serengeti
Where the scavengers circle and wait
Two lions were spurned by the friends they grew up with
For choosing the wrong sort of mate

"It goes against nature," the other beasts jeered
As they cast them out onto the plain
"Wherever two lions are falling in love
There should only be one with a mane."

Their hearts full of sadness, the two lions left
They wandered for days and for weeks
Wondering whether their love for each other
Was the love of unnatural freaks

Till at last they met others just like them
As they stopped for a drink at a stream
To the two lions banished for loving each other
It felt like a magical dream

As the love that, once, could not be spoken
Became love that will not be denied
And they banded together, a new kind of family
Now that's what I call a gay pride.

Excuses

It wasn't my fault
You don't understand
I fell off my chair
It slipped out of my hand

I just didn't see it
It got in my way
Someone else did it
He said it was okay

It was like that already
Well, what else could I do?
I forgot
But you *said!*
They're *lying!*
It's *true!*

It wasn't my fault
I wasn't even there
You're not listening!
IT'S NOT FAIR!

43

I Did Do My Homework

I did do my homework,
I did it last night
and I'm fairly convinced
I got most of it right.
But along came a shark,
a quite hungry Great White –
and it swallowed my homework completely.

"You can't do that!" I said,
catching hold of its fin.
"I just did!" said the shark,
with a villainous grin.
Then it opened its jaws
saying, "Won't you come in?"
and it swallowed me too, rather neatly.

Which appeared to me
unnecessarily cruel.
As you can imagine
I feel such a fool,
for in this situation
I can't go to school
and I'm wondering quite what the use is,

as I'm sitting here, bored
and alone in the dark.
I can't hand in my homework
from inside a shark
and there's nobody here
who can give it a mark.
So I'm phoning to give my excuses.

Blank Verse

I was going to write a poem
About my mind going blank
But I couldn't think of one.

The World is Too Much, Sometimes

The world is too much, sometimes
For fragile minds to bear
They need to hide, like frightened mice
Who know the cat is there.

When everything is going well
It's easy to be strong
But everybody has a time
When everything is wrong.

And each of us is fragile
When our world starts to collapse
We need more understanding
Than we sometimes get, perhaps.

It makes it worse to mock and curse
Or greet with scornful laughter
Someone whose only trespass
Is to need some looking after.

And though we cannot all take care
Of every fragile mind
Still, we can do our best, each day
In trying to be kind.

Rainbows and Steel

There's a story I've heard from the birds and the bees
From the oceans and mountains, the grass and the trees
From the lion and lamb, from the shark and the seal
Of a woman who's made out of rainbows and steel

Though the hues of her haloes are gentle and warm
They're formed by the light that shines out of the storm
And she stands with a strength that those colours conceal
The woman who's made out of rainbows and steel

She's a goddess of war and a herald of peace
She brings prisoners comfort and captives release
And in chains at her feet shall her enemies kneel
The woman who's made out of rainbows and steel

So when life is a tempest that tears at the skies
And the world is a whirl of deception and lies
Just pray that the thunderclouds part to reveal
The woman who's made out of rainbows and steel.

Snowfall

I woke in the night
Saw the snow settling
In the garden, remaking itself
Inch by inch
Inch by inch

It shone in the moonlight
A soft reflection
Of a soft reflection

As the down-like feathers of snow
Came down, like feathers of snow

I Am a Man of Naughtiness

I am a man of naughtiness
My name is Mr Poo
I like to do all sorts of things
I really shouldn't do

I like to run with scissors
I like to pick my nose
I like to walk into a shop
And take off all my clothes

I like to shout "Bananas!"
At people who are thinking
I like to run around a ship
Pretending that's it's sinking

I like to tickle centipedes
I like to juggle bread
I like to steal an elephant
And hide it in your bed

But quite the very naughtiest
Of all the things I do
Is telling lies in poetry

For none of this is true.

Limerick Written by a Dog

Woof woof woof woof woof woof woof woof woof
Woof woof woof woof woof woof woof woof woof
Woof woof woof woof bark
Woof woof woof woof bark
Woof woof woof woof woof woof woof woof woof

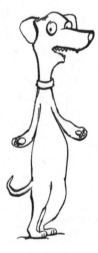

A Serious and Thought-Provoking Poem. Written by a Dog

Woof
Woof woof woof
Woof woof woof woof woof
Woof woof
Woof woof woof woof
Woof woof woof woof woof woof
Woof woof
Woof woof
Woof woof

Miaow.

If I were a bear

If I were a bear, I would not be prepared
To live in a cave and to hunt and to forage
If I were a bear, I would really prefer
To live in a house in the woods and eat porridge.

Let Down Your Hair

Why did Rapunzel
let down her hair
to be climbed by the Prince who was waiting out there?
Why did she let him
ascend to the top
without yelling, "That's really sore! Ow! Get down!
STOP!!!"
And why, if he wanted
to see her again
did he not think of something to cause her less pain?
If he'd wanted to make her
a little bit gladder
he'd have galloped off home and returned with a ladder.

If I was Rapunzel
and I'd heard the Prince ask it
I'd have let down my hair in return for a basket.
I'd have said, if he wanted
to make me his wife
he should place in the basket a very sharp knife.
I'd have pulled up the basket,
chopped off my hair,
climbed down to the Prince who was waiting out there,
said, "Thanks for your help,"
shaken his hand
and gone off to check out the lie of the land.

Whoever the Prince,
you don't want to marry him
if he needlessly hurts you
or expects you to carry him.

If Somebody Hurts You

If somebody hurts you, then tell.
There isn't a value to silence.
The person who hurts you, then says it's a secret,
is just adding violence to violence.

If somebody makes you feel bad,
don't let them pretend that it's fun.
For cruelty hidden, disguised as a joke,
is still cruelty, cruelly done.

If somebody threatens you, tell.
It's your way of taking control.
Better the bruise they may leave on your body
than the one they might leave on your soul.

Don't be afraid to get help.
Remember, and know this is true:
your silence is useful to no one at all
except those who are picking on you.

How to Write a Cinquain

Cinquain
Two syllables
Then four, six, eight, and two
Name, description, action, feeling
Cinquain

Dry Leaf

Dry leaf
Pale, brittle, brown
Waiting to feed the earth
To give its life one last meaning
Dry leaf

I Would Not Like to Be a Slug

I would not like to be a slug
I think it would be icky
For slugs are stretchy, slimy, squishy
Slithery and sticky

But if I were a gastropod
I think that on reflection
I'd rather be a slimy snail
At least I'd have protection
From birds and dogs and cats, though not
From loathing and rejection.

Robinswood Hill

On Robinswood Hill there's a parrot.
They think it escaped from a cage
in someone's house, perhaps,
and made its home up there
among the trees.

If you climb the hill, through the woods,
you can see it sometimes.
A vivid flash of blue and gold among the leafy green.

Do you think the other birds are jealous?
Do they resent this colourful stranger?
Or are they glad to have it there, its brightness standing
out like summer sunlight
against the blacks and browns and greys
of their own autumnal feathering?

Unexpected Item

For a supermarket auto-till, there's really nothing scarier
Than an unexpected item lurking in the bagging area
And likewise, for a poet, there is little that is worse
Than an unexpected letter in the last line of the versel.

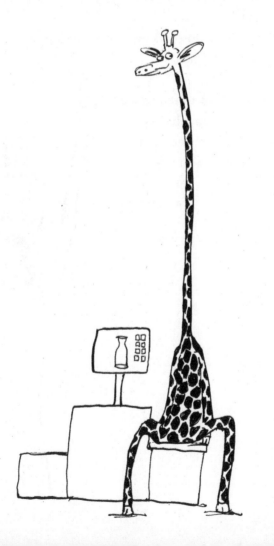

Boys Will Be Boys

"It's in their nature," so they always tell us.
"Boys will be boys."
And then to us, they say, "Be kind.
Be gentle. Make less noise.
It isn't ladylike to be so rough.
No, not at all.
Don't be so loud. Don't take up so much room.
Make yourselves small."

But I wonder what would happen
if they made the boys be quiet
and told us all it was nature's way
for the girls to cause a riot.

There is a Poem

There is a poem
On the tip of my tongue
On the tips of my fingers
In the tip of my mind
And if I shut out the world
And concentrate
Maybe I'll catch it
Say it
Write it down
Maybe I'll feel it
Maybe I'll know it
Maybe I'll hold it
Maybe I'll grow it

There is a poem

There is a poem.

Onomatopoeia Poem

Onomatopitter-patter, rain against the window spatters
Onomatopop-and-splatter, burst balloon as liquid scatters
Onomatopeep-and-quack, ducklings calling, mother
    answers
Onomatoclick-and-clack and tap and shuffle, feet of
    dancers
Onomatobiff-and-bonk, onomatoclick-and-clonk
Onomatoping-and-bang, onomatozing-and-clang
Onomatocroak-of-frog or buzzing of a bumblebee
Filling up the world around us
Onomatopoetry.

The Dog's Not Allowed
on the Chair

The dog's not allowed on the chair
Which he thinks is extremely unfair
But we don't want it covered with mud and with hair
So the dog's not allowed on the chair

The dog's not allowed on the chair
Which is more than the poor thing can bear
So he gazes up sadly and howls with despair
For the dog's not allowed on the chair

The dog's not allowed on the chair
Which he's cross that the humans won't share
It's enough, were he able, to make the dog swear
For the dog's not allowed on the chair

Though the dog's not allowed on the chair
Now he reckons he just doesn't care
For he's brought home his friend, who's a grizzly bear
And they're both taking turns on the chair

While the family enjoys the fresh air.

Computer Problems

It's just a littl problm
But it's driving m brsrk
I spilld coff on my kyboard
Now my lttr won't work

And almost as annoying
I suppos it's just my luck –
Is that vry now and thn
On of the othr kys gts stuckkkkkkkkkkkkkkkkkkkkkkkkkkkkk
kkkkkkkkkkkkkkkkkkkkkkkkkkkkkkkkkkkkkkkkkkkkkkkkkkkkkk
kkkkkkkkkkkkkkkkkkkkkkkkkkkkkkkkkkkkkkkkkkkkkkkkkkkkkk
kkkkkkkkkkkkkkkkkkkkkkkkkkkkkkkkkkkkkkkkkkkkkkkkkkkkkk
kkkkkkkkkkkkkkkkkkkkkkkkkkkkkkkkkkkkkkkkkkkkkkkkkkkkkk
kkkkkkkkkkkkkkkkkkkkkkkkkkkkkkkkkkkkkkkkkkkkkkkkkkkkkk
kkkkkkkkkkkkkkkkkkkkkkkkkkkkkkkkkkkkkkkkkkkkkkkkkkkkkk
kkkkkkkkkkkkkkkkkkkkkkkkkkkkkkkkkkkkkkkkkkkkkkkkkkkkkk
kkkkkkkkkkkkkkkkkkkkkkkkkkkkkkkkkkkkkkkkkkkkkkkkkkkkkk
kkkkkkkkkkkkkkkkkkkkkkkkkkkkkkkkkkkkkkkkkkkkkkkkkkkkkk
kkkkkkkkkkkkkkkkkkkkkkkkkkkkkkkkkkkkkkkkkkkkkkkkkkkkkk
kkkkkkkkkkkkkkkkkkkkkkkkkkkkkkkkkkkkkkkkkkkkkkkkkkkkkk
kkkkkkkkkkkkkkkkkkkkkkkkkkkkkkkkkkkkkkkkkkkkkkkkkkkkkk
kkkkkkkkkkkkkkkkkkkkkkkkkkkkkkkkkkkkkkkkkkkkkkkkkkkkkk
kkkkkkkkkkkkkkkkkkkkkkkkkkkkkkkkkkkkkkkkkkkkkkkkkkkkkk
kkkkkkkkkkkkkkkkkkkkkkkkkkkkkkkkkkkkkkkkkkkkkkkkkkkkkk
kkkkkkkkkkkkkkkkkkkkkkkkkkkkkkkkkkkkkkkkkkkkkkkkkkkkkk
kkkkkkkkkkkkkkkkkkkkkkkkkkkkkkkkkkkkkkkkkkkkkkkkkkkkkk

Pity the Bat

Pity the bat
Who can't wear a hat
Even on days when it's snowing
For a bat, it appears
If it covers its ears
Is unable to hear where it's going

The Problem with Acrostics

Acrostic poems make me
Cross sometimes, because
Really when you write a poem you should be focusing
On choosing the right words, not on the letters that go at the
Start of
The line, which can lead to lines beginning
In the wrong places and
Containing the wrong words.

Perhaps we should
Only write an acrostic when it's the best way to
Express what we want to say. I think that would
Make sense.

Steps

Sturdy
Terraced
Earthen
Pathway
Somewhere

What Kind of Poem Is This?

Annoyed, irritated, vexed at being

Cut from the branch
Ripped from the bough
Or torn from the tree.
Seething at the hand that
Scoops it from the ground

Sticks it in a bundle
Takes it home.
If it could, it would bark in fury, for it knows it's been
Collected to be fuel
Kindling for the fire; and angrily, it awaits its fate.

Our Minds Are Made of Play-Dough

Our minds are made of play-dough.
They arrive in fresh, bright colours
ready to be shaped
and shaped
and shaped again.
To be stretched,
even, sometimes, snapped
and squished back together, gleefully rolled
into a joyful ball, or brick, or blob.
A pancake or a sausage.

They need to be kneaded,
massaged and pummelled,
mixed up with other colours and, most of all,
played with.

Left alone, ignored, neglected,
they become dry, brittle.
They crack and crumble,
harden, until
they lock into a rigid, single shape, their purpose gone,
or turn to useless grit.

Play with your mind.
Enjoy it
Stretch it
Add to it.

Use it.

Cough

I'd like to tell this stupid cough
Go take a hike. Get lost. Back ough.

I've had much more than just enough
Of all this slimy phlegmy stough

Expectorating from my chest
At times that I do not think best

I'd like to tell this coff: we're through.
Back off. I've had enough of yough.

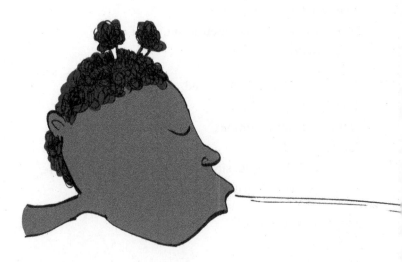

Calorie Morality

Mum says to Dad,
"I've been really good today:
hardly any breakfast,
no snacks,
just an apple for lunch –
and look! A small portion now, too."

Mum says to me,
"Be a good boy:
eat up all your dinner
or you won't get any pudding."

Zoos - Good or Bad?

Animals
Do not choose
To live in zoos
Put yourself in their shoes:
In captivity
From nativity
Immensely restricted in their choice of activity
On display
Every day
Walls and bars to make them stay
Until the end.
I can't pretend.
It's not a life I'd recommend.

And yet
Let's not forget
The work of zoos, the goals they set
In education
Conservation
Saving animals from eradication
Keeping them alive
Helping them to thrive
Ensuring that endangered species survive.

Do you think it's true
That the zoo
Can be a bad thing, and a good thing, too?

In the Library

In the library
A shelf. On the shelf, a book
In the book, a world

·QUIET PLEASE·

Poet

A poet, standing in a field
Turning to words what the world has revealed.

Goodbye, Grandad

Goodbye, Grandad.
Let's not talk about the things we never did,

the unwalked hills, the unfished streams,
the unscored goals, the unshared dreams,
the things we always meant to do.

Instead, let me sit here
quietly
by your bedside
and stroke your hair, and hold your hand
as you did for me

when I was small.

Learning to Walk

You'll never learn to walk or run
Unless you learn to fall
The only ones who make no mistakes
Are those who do nothing at all

The First Time I Went to Scotland

The first time I went to Scotland, it was on a trip,
a holiday
with lots of other kids
from schools all over Northern Ireland.

The first evening we were there
the people in charge took us into town
and said,
"Off you go. Have fun; see the shops.
Buy some wee presents to take home to your families
and we'll see you back here at the coach in two hours."

Off we went, in twos and threes and fours.
I was with my new friend Simon
and someone else, I think.
Richard, maybe, or Andrew.
We went into the wee sweetshops
and the wee souvenir shops
and all the other wee shops,
looking for sweets we didn't have back home
and little Scottish gifts our parents might like.

But there was one shop in the middle of town that was
just a bit bigger than the others.
Not like a supermarket or a department store
but bigger than the wee shops.
I was talking with Simon
and Andrew, or was it Richard,
as we went in.

I went first
through the door, chatting away
and
without thinking
I stopped just inside the doorway
and lifted my arms
just a bit away from my body.

Y'see, back then in Northern Ireland
there were people,
bad people,
who would make bombs,
And sometimes they would go into a shop
and leave a bomb hidden somewhere
and go away,
and the shop would blow up.
Bang.
No more shop.

And sometimes
if there were people in the shop
no more them, either.

So if a shop could afford it,
the owner would pay someone
to stand inside the door
and search people as they came in.
"Lift up your arms, please."
And pat, pat, pat they'd go
all down your sides,
your back,
your tummy,
your legs,
making sure you had nothing hidden in your clothes
that might be a bomb.

Yes, even kids.

They even searched kids.

I must have been so used to it
I did it without thinking.
Lifted my arms
and waited to be searched.

But in Scotland, they didn't do that.
So I was just standing there
with my arms in the air,
blocking the doorway
for no reason.

It took me a moment to realise,
then I felt a bit stupid.

When we got back to the coach
I almost didn't say,
because I felt embarrassed
about standing there
waiting to be searched
when no one was there to search me.

But I needn't have worried, because
it turned out
most of the others had done the same thing
in the same shop.

I wonder what the woman at the counter thought?

Taking my Children to Larne

When Noah and Cara were teenagers
I took them on holiday to Northern Ireland.
And because they wanted to see where I grew up
We went to Larne.

We visited my old school.
We drove up the road I used to live in,
talked to one of my old neighbours

and walked along the Main Street
looking at all the shops I used to know.

A lot of them had changed since I lived there.
"That used to be Woolworths," I said.
"And across the road was Wellworths.
Over there, that was the King's Arms
and this shop here,
I'm sure this one was Alexander's, the toy shop.
It got blown up a couple of times..."

They both burst out laughing.

"What's so funny?" I said.

"You," they told me. "You just said
It got blown up a couple of times
as if that was normal."

And I laughed too,
though somewhere inside, I was thinking,
"But it was.
It was."

Yellow Group

Kylie's full of energy, she won't do things by half
Salman's Mr Fun and Games, he always makes us laugh
And Seema's singing voice is sweet, and clear as any bell
But in class we're just the Yellow Group, who don't know
    how to spell.

Faye can tell you all about the planets, if you'll let her
Femi brought a wounded squirrel home, and made it
    better
And Josh can make up stories that are thrilling and
    exciting
But in class we're just the Yellow Group, who aren't much
    good at writing.

Salman's great at somersaults, he's really quite gymnastic
The superhero pictures Femi draws are just fantastic
And Faye, the way she dances, should be on the television
But in class we're just the Yellow Group, who still can't do
    division.

I'm not bad at basketball, and Seema's good at running
The skateboard tricks that Josh can do are absolutely
    stunning
And nobody I know can climb a tree as fast as Kylie
But in class we're just the Yellow Group, who no one rates
    too highly.

So if you talk to Yellow Group, you'll very quickly find
That all of us are talented and all of us are kind
And knowing this the way I do, I sometimes wonder sadly
Why the things that make us Yellow Group are the things
    that we do badly.

You are You

You are you
And that's okay
Small or tall
Straight or gay
Fat or thin
Short hair or long
You are you
And you belong.

Whatever the colour
Of skin or of hair
Whatever you like
And whatever you wear
Do no harm. Try to love
And please know this is true:
You're important. You matter.

It's okay to be you.

About the Poet and the Illustrator

John Dougherty

was born in Larne, Northern Ireland, and some of the poems in this collection reflect his childhood there. He became a primary teacher, but is now a full-time writer and performer, with over 40 books published. He is a favourite visitor to school and library workshops and has performed at book fairs and festivals from Swindon to Sydney. His first book for Otter-Barry Books was *Dinosaurs and Dinner-Ladies*. He lives in Stroud, Gloucestershire.

Tom Morgan-Jones

is a dip-pen illustrator. He has illustrated over 75 books for children (he's also had his work appear on the side of milk cartons, on top of cakes, all over satirical board games, inside museums and newspapers, on the outside of schools, behind bands and poets, on chocolate bars and the back of buses and all the way around tins of dog biscuits and Norway's National football stadium). He loves mark making, he loves drawing, he loves illustrating and he loves story telling. He is the illustrator of *Dinosaurs and Dinner-Ladies* for Otter-Barry Books. He lives in Edinburgh, Scotland.